5 Christmas Plays for children

Abingdon Press

CONTENTS

CHRISTMAS? BAH HUMBUG!

By Shirley Lockhart Ingram

Production Notes

Scrooge Jr. doesn't understand the reason for Christmas celebrations. A group of children share their understanding of Christmas through word, carols, and scripture. Scrooge's heart is touched and he realizes that the birth of a tiny baby so long ago is still important to us today.

Props

A stool for Scrooge Jr.
A manger
Small chair or stool for Mary
Nine large cards for the letter of Christmas

Characters

Scrooge Jr. *(older youth or young adult)*
Nine *(or more)* **children**
Scripture Reader
Mary
Joseph
Shepherds *(any number)*
Angel *(optional)*

SCROOGE JR.	*(enters, shuffling his feet, head down, mumbling)* Too much shopping . . . too much money spent on people I don't really like . . . too many parties . . . stores too crowded, push and shove *(gestures).* . . a Christmas tree . . . Bah, humbug! *(Moves to one side, sits on a stool.)*
CHILDREN;	*(enter from the rear singing. They should walk down the aisle singing, "Good Christian Friends [Men] Rejoice." Once they have reached the altar area, they may stand and sing other familiar songs, such as "Away in a Manger." Turning to Scrooge Jr, they sing, "We Wish You a Merry Christmas.")*

5

SCROOGE:	*(rising from his seat)* Merry Christmas? Bah Humbug! Don't know why you are so jolly. It's just another time of the year. People are hurrying around, pushing and shoving . . . driving too fast . . . eating too much. Bah Humbug!
CHILD:	I'm sorry you feel that way. Listen to this carol and perhaps it will tell you why we are so joyful.
	Children sing "Go Tell It On the Mountain."
SCROOGE JR:	No, I still don't see it. Christmas is just about someone born a long time ago. It doesn't make any difference to me. It's a waste of time and money.
CHILD:	Maybe if we explained the letters of Christmas, you'd understand. May we?
SCROOGE JR.	*(impatient)* Well, I guess. Go ahead.
	Nine children line up, each holding one letter from the word CHRISTMAS.
FIRST CHILD:	C – Christ Jesus has come from Heaven.
SECOND CHILD:	H – Holy Son of God.
THIRD CHILD:	R – Righteous and pure.
FOURTH CHILD:	I – An infant born in a stable.
FIFTH CHILD:	S – A star which shone so bright.
SIXTH CHILD:	T - Tidings of joy to all people on earth.
SEVENTH CHILD:	M - a lowly manger where Baby Jesus slept.
EIGHTH CHILD:	A – Angels that sang that night.

NINTH CHILD: S – A savior sent from heaven, a shepherd for his people, the Son of God.

ALL: Christmas! Christmas!

CHILD: These letters spell Christmas. They tell us that God loves everyone. "God so loved the world that he sent his only begotten son, that whosoever believeth in him, should not perish, but have everlasting life." (John 3: 16 KJV)

SCROOGE JR. Say, isn't that John 3:16? I learned that a long time ago, when I went to Sunday School. *(repeats the verse and stares into space)*

CHILD: That's the meaning of Christmas. God sent Jesus into the world as a tiny baby to tell of God's love for all people. The poor shepherds were the first to hear the good news, and they shared it with others. Wise men traveled from far away to honor him with gifts. Jesus was the first and best Christmas gift. He promised eternal life for all people everywhere.

SCROOGE JR: Well . . this sort of makes sense. Sounds like Christmas was a miracle, but how to you know all this is real?

CHILD: Do you believe in the Bible?

SCROOGE JR.: Yes . . . I guess so. It was important to me a long time ago.

CHILD: Then listen to the story told in the second chapter of Luke, verses 1-20.

BIBLE READER: Reads Luke 2:1-10.

7

(As the Bible Reader reads, the characters of Mary and Joseph walk down the aisle and take their place around the manger. The shepherds enter, kneel and leave. As the reading comes to an end, Mary and Joseph exit.)

SCROOGE JR. *(rubs his eyes)* Say . . . have I been dreaming? It's almost like I was there in Bethlehem. The birth of Jesus did happen, didn't it?

CHILD: Yes, over 2000 years ago in Bethlehem.

SCROOGE JR. *(all smiles)* Yes, I do believe. I believe in the miracle! Jesus came to earth for me! Thanks for helping me believe. *(shakes a few children's hands)* Why don't we shout the Good News to everyone? What's that song about telling everyone?

CHILDREN: "Go Tell It On the Mountain?"

SCROOGE JR.: Yes. That's it. Let me sing it with you.

CHILDREN AND
SCROOGE JR. *sing* "Go tell It On the Mountain."

Nativity characters enter and recreate the manger scene.

SCROOGE JR. *(To congregation)* Please join us in singing "Joy to the World."

EVERYWHERE, EVERYWHERE, CHRISTMAS TONIGHT

By Shirley Lockhart Ingram

Production notes

This play can be adapted in many ways. If you are blessed with many children, the speaking parts can be divided into two parts for the international children; if you do not have enough children, some characters can be omitted.

Costumes

International children should be dressed according to their traditional cultural attire. Consult an encyclopedia for help. ***MISS TRADITION*** *should wear a flowing dress and a tinsel wreath on her head.* **Mary** *and* **JOSEPH** *can wear typical biblical costumes.*

Props

a log *(small enough for a child to carry)*
a big Christmas card
table-top size Christmas tree, poinsettia plant, a wooden shoe,
assorted bells, miniature manger scene, a world globe.

Characters

Two American Children
Miss Tradition
Two English Children
German Child
Mexican Child
Dutch Child
Chinese Child
Italian Child
Mary
Joseph

Children enter singing "Deck the Halls." They come down the center aisle and gather at the left side of the chancel area. They may stand or sit. The two American children step out to the center.

FIRST AMERICAN
CHILD: I like that Christmas carol, don't you?

SECOND AMERICAN
CHILD: Yes, I do. Is it an old carol? Like older than my grandmother?

FIRST AMERICAN
CHILD: I don't know. Maybe we . . .

               Miss Tradition *has entered from a side door and has been listening. The children look startled when she speaks.*

MISS
TRADITION: Maybe I can help.

FIRST AMERICAN
CHILD: Oh, who are you?

MISS
TRADITION: I am Miss Christmas Tradition. I represent all the customs and traditions that we observe and celebrate at this time of the year.

SECOND AMERICAN
CHILD: What do you mean represent? We've always had these customs haven't we?

FIRST AMERICAN
CHILD: Don't our families give us our customs?

MISS
TRADITION: Well, let's think about some of them. I'm glad you're interested in our customs. Many of our customs originated in other countries. They have been passed down to us today through our families or our churches. People from all around the world (*points to globe*) share in this celebration of love and joy. Let's ask some of the children from other countries to tell us about their traditions.

(**American Children** *move to one side and sit*)

Two **English Children** *step forward. The first is carrying a large stick of wood.*

FIRST ENGLISH
CHILD: We're from England. One of our customs is the yule log. This piece of wood represents the yule log.

MISS
TRADITION: Yes, that's right. A yule log is really very big. It would burn in the fireplace for many days. The custom of burning the Yule Log came from the Norse and the Anglo-Saxons. They believed burning the log would take away the evil from the previous year. After they became Christians, the Yule log became part of their Christmas traditions. Today we enjoy sitting with our families and watching the flames in a fireplace. We can think about the shepherds gathered around their fires on the night of Jesus' birth. (*turns to second child*) Do you have a custom to share with us?

SECOND ENGLISH

CHILD: Another custom from England is sending Christmas cards. The first Christmas card *(holds up a big card)* was believed to have been sent in London, England, in 1846.

MISS

TRADITION: Also England's Charles Dickens wrote the famous story, "A Christmas Carol" about Scrooge and Tiny Tim. So, it's Christmas in merry ol' England.

*(**English Children** return to the group.)*

ALL CHILDREN: *(Sing,* "Everywhere, Everywhere, Christmas Tonight.")

MISS

TRADITION: So true! Everywhere, it's Christmas. Let's find out what customs come from Germany. *(**German Child** steps forward, carrying a small decorated tree.)* What do you have to share with us?

GERMAN

CHILD: Many people believe that Martin Luther from Germany was the first person to bring a tree inside the house. He was walking through the woods one night and saw the light from stars glistening on fir trees. He though how beautiful a tree would be with lights, so he brought the tree home and put candles on it. His children decorated it and were delighted with the tree. They ran and placed their gifts under it.

MISS

TRADITION: So we have Martin Luther to thank for our Christmas tree custom. Let's sing a German carol we often hear at this time of the year.

ALL CHILDREN: *(Sing, "O Christmas Tree.")*

MISS TRADITION: Do you know the German word for Christmas tree?

GERMAN CHILD: "Tannebaum." Some people use that word when they sing this song. *(sits down tree and exits)*

MISS TRADITION: Thank you. "Silent Night" was also written by a German pastor, Franz Gruber, in 1818. It's now a favorite carol. *(turns to congregation)* Won't you join us in singing this wonderful carol?

Cast and congregation sing. As the sounds of the hymn fade away, "Feliz Navidad" can be heard.

MISS TRADITION: That sounds like music from Mexico.

MEXICAN CHILD: *(steps forward, carrying a poinsettia plant)* I'm from Mexico, which is below the United States. In Mexico we celebrate Christmas from December 6 to January 6.

MISS TRADITION: Tell us about the plant you are carrying.

MEXICAN CHILD: This is a poinsettia plant; (holds up plant) its leaves are shaped like a flaming red star to remind us of the star of Bethlehem.

MISS TRADITION:	Legend has it that a little girl had no gift to take to church on Christmas Eve. Coming upon a plant growing beside the road, she picked it and took it to leave at the altar. When she knelt and laid her gift at the altar, the leaves suddenly turned into the beautiful plant we see here.
MEXICAN CHILD:	*(adds the poinsettia plant to the display and returns to the other children)*
ALL CHILDREN:	*(Sing* "Feliz Navidad."*)*
MISS TRADITION:	What does *Feliz Navidad* mean?
ALL CHILDREN:	Merry Christmas.
MISS TRADITION:	What other customs do we have?
DUTCH CHILD:	I'm from Holland. We celebrate St. Nicholas Day on December 6. St. Nicholas was a bishop in Asia Minor. He was very generous and shared what he had in secret.
MISS TRADITION:	Where did he leave the gifts?
DUTCH CHILD:	In stockings or shoes. We leave out wooden shoes today while other people hang stockings.

**MISS
TRADITION:** In America, what do we call him?

**AMERICAN
CHILDREN:** *(stand up and answer)* Santa Claus!

Dutch Child *adds shoe to display and rejoins other children. Sound of bells ringing.*

**MISS
TRADITION:** Does anyone hear bells ringing?

ALL CHILDREN: Yes.

CHINESE CHILD: *(Walks up to center of stage.)* I'm from China. Bells have been used in China to call people to worship for centuries.

**MISS
TRADITION:** Now big church bells ring for Christmas Eve and Christmas Day services in many countries. We hear a lot of bells during the Christmas season don't we—church bells, sleigh bells, bells rung on street corners. Does anyone know a carol about bells?

CHINESE CHILD: "I Heard the Bells on Christmas Day."

**MISS
TRADITION:** That's right! Henry Wadsworth Longfellow wrote that special carol. Let's sing it together.

ALL CHILDREN: *(sing "I Heard the Bells on Christmas Day.")*

**MISS
TRADITION:** What a lovely song! *(pause and look around)*

The real meaning of Christmas is portrayed in a very special way that originated in Italy. Can anyone tell me about that?

ITALIAN CHILD: I'm from Italy. We've been told that St. Francis of Assisi arranged the very first nativity or manger scene in Italy. Because so many people could not read, he set up a manger scene in the village square. He used live animals and he may have used people from the village. Many, many people came to hear about the birth of Jesus.

MISS
TRADITION: When did this first manger scene take place?

ITALIAN CHILD: Probably in the thirteenth century.

MISS
TRADITION: Now churches and families all over the world use nativity scenes to share the miracle of Jesus' birth. Many people do not place the Christ Child in the manger until Christmas Eve.

ALL CHILDREN: *(sing, "Everywhere, Everywhere, Christmas Tonight.")*

MISS
TRADITION: *(stands and motions all children to join her)* People all over the world observe the spirit of Christmas in many different ways, but what is the one thing that never changes?

ALL CHILDREN: We celebrate because Jesus was born!

MISS
TRADITION: That's right! Who would think that news of a child's birth 2000 years ago would have

spread around the world from a stable in Bethlehem? As we think about this wonderful event, let's share our joy by singing "Joy to the World."

CHILDREN AND

CONGREGATION: "Joy to the World." *(As the hymn is sung, Mary and Joseph quietly enter and stroll down the aisle and kneel by the manger. If you wish you can add shepherds and angels.)*

CHRISTMAS HIDE AND SEEK

By Barbara T. Rowland

Production Notes

This is a play for children in grades one through three. It may be done as is or used for a "do-it-yourself" choir musical. Simply insert your choice of music after each scene. Children playing parts step out of the choir and in front of it for lines. If you are doing the play without music, children playing the scenes may stand with their backs to the congregation until the searchers come to them. Arrange the scenes stage right to left across the platform.

Cast in order of appearance:

Seeker 1 and Seeker 2 *(may be boys or girls; everyday clothes)*

Mother *(girl; wears apron and holds bowl and spoon)*

Christmas Present
(child with wrapping paper over clothes; bow on head)

Charity Box
(child with arms and legs through big box marked "Charity")

Joseph, Mary *(boy and girl in biblical dress)*

Grandmother *(girl with shawl and glasses, holding Bible)*

Scene 1
(Scene may be preceded by music)

SEEKER 1:	Why do you look so sad? It's almost Christmas!
SEEKER 2:	That's the problem. I heard Grandmother say Christmas is lost!
SEEKER 1:	Lost? Christmas? I don't believe it. It must be hiding somewhere!

SEEKER 2:	(*brightens*) Hey! Maybe so. Let's look for it.
SEEKER 1:	O. K. Where should we look?
SEEKER 2:	(*thinks*) Oh, I know! Let's look in the kitchen where Mother is cooking.
	(*Approach **Mother** who steps out of choir or turns around.*)
SEEKER 2:	Mother! Is Christmas here where you're cooking?
MOTHER:	I'm making cookies and cakes For our family and relations. But this isn't Christmas, dears, Its a PART of our celebration.
	(*Music reflecting secular holiday season*)

Scene 2

SEEKER 1:	Christmas is still lost—or hiding. Where else can we look?
SEEKER 2:	I have an idea. Maybe its under our decorated tree.
SEEKER 1:	Let's go see.
	(*Seekers approach **Christmas Present** who steps out of choir or turns around.*)
SEEKER 2:	We're looking for Christmas. Can you help us?
SEEKER 1:	Are you hiding Christmas all wrapped up in a big box?

**CHRISTMAS
PRESENT:**   I'm not telling what's inside me
'cause I'm a present for a friend.
People give lots of gifts, you see.
But Christmas isn't what they send.

(Music reflecting giving gifts or celebrating.)

Scene 3

SEEKER 1:   So Christmas isn't hiding in the kitchen with the cooking or under the tree with the presents.

SEEKER 2:   We just have to keep looking. Surely it's around here somewhere.

SEEKER 1:   Say, I know where there's a box we put things to give away at Christmas. Maybe that's where Christmas is!

SEEKER 2:   Good idea. Let's go look for it there.

*(Approach **Charity Box** who steps out of choir or turns around.)*

SEEKER 1:   We're looking everywhere for Christmas.

SEEKER 2:   Do you have Christmas in your box?

CHARITY BOX: I hold lots of good food and toys
As well as hats, gloves, and jeans.
But giving things to girls and boys
Isn't all that Christmas means.

(Music reflecting season as good time of year.)

Scene 4

SEEKER 1: Christmas isn't hiding in the give-away box. I'm getting tired of looking!

SEEKER 2: Wait! Why didn't I think of this before!

SEEKER 1: What?

SEEKER 2: I know where there's a yard with a manger scene in it—you know, Mary, and Joseph, and Baby Jesus. Maybe Christmas is there!

SEEKER 1: Let's go see!

(Seekers approach Nativity scene. Actors turn around)

SEEKER 1: Excuse me, Mr. Joseph. We heard Grandmother say Christmas is lost and we're seeking it.

SEEKER 2: Is it hidden here with you?

JOSEPH: We're here to remind everyone
Of the great gift God sent.
But you can know what was done
And miss the meaning of the event.

(Music such as "Away in a Manger.")

Scene 5

SEEKER 2: It doesn't sound like Christmas is hiding in the manger after all. I thought for sure that's where it would be.

SEEKER 1: I know, let's go ask Grandmother. She was the one talking about Christmas being lost. Maybe she knows where to look.

SEEKER 2: Great idea. Let's go see Gran.

*(Seekers approach **Grandmother** who steps out of the choir or turns around.)*

SEEKER 2: Gran, I heard you talking to Granddad about Christmas being lost. We've looked everywhere and can't find it.

SEEKER 1: Do you have any idea where we can look? We must find it!

GRANDMOTHER: Oh dear children, that isn't what I meant. Christmas means Jesus and our salvation. Our worship of God for the Son God sent Sometimes gets lost in our celebration!

SEEKER 1: So, Christmas isn't really lost?

SEEKER 2: But we can miss thanking God for that special gift?

GRANDMOTHER: You are right! You only have to look in your heart!

SEEKER 1: So Christmas isn't hiding. It can happen to me in my heart!

SEEKER 2: I hope everyone seeks Christmas and finds it.

(Joyous Christmas music.)

THE BIRTHDAY GIFTS

by Barbara T. Rowland

Production Notes

This is a Christmas play for children in grades four through six. It may be used as a choir musical. The number of children may vary by assigning lines as determined by the director. (There are about 50 lines other than the lines for the three children having the party. You may use five children with ten lines or ten children with five lines and so on.) The set requires varied seating for the children. The room may be a family room with a Christmas tree.

Main characters

Ellen
Nathan
Dan

Children enter and go to platform singing "Happy Birthday" to Jesus. General laughter as they fall into a variety of seats or sit on the floor.

CHILD: Hey Ellen, this was a good idea—to have a birthday party for Jesus!

CHILD: Yeah. I talk a lot about what I want for Christmas—

CHILD: Forgetting whose birthday it is, huh? So do I.

ELLEN: Well, that's why we thought about this party. When we have birthdays we ask friends to come celebrate with us.

CHILD: So, you asked us to have a party for Jesus.

CHILD: Cool. That was really a good cake you made for Jesus' birthday!

CHILD:	Yeah. Chocolate is my favorite.
CHILD:	And I like my tree ornament favor you gave us. This little star will go on my tree this Christmas! *(holds up ornament)* Thanks.
CHILD:	But, when we come to each other's birthday parties, we bring presents. What can we give to Jesus?
CHILD:	When his Father owns the whole world!
CHILD:	Guess that includes all the video games—
CHILD:	And ice skates—
CHILD:	And bikes—
CHILD:	You guys are crazy. Jesus doesn't want that stuff!
CHILD:	Well, what does he want?
ELLEN:	My brothers and I thought about that. Mama helped us get some presents ready. Want to see?
	(Chorus of "Sure" "Let's see" and "What are they?" Ellen runs to get a big wrapped box at one side of the platform or from under the Christmas tree and brings it to the center of the group.)
ELLEN:	This is the first gift Jesus wants. It's "Praise and Worship." See the label on the side? Here's a verse I wrote to to with it:

We praise God in prayer,
In scripture and in song.
We thank God for his care
And worship God alone.

CHILD:	Hey, I like that! But what's in the box?

CHILD: How can you put praise and worship in a box?

ELLEN: Well, you can't really. But I put in things to remind us of the gift of praise. Look at this *(lifts out hymnal and holds it up)*.

CHILD: That's our song book! And it has praise and worship music in it!

CHILD: Cool. And some of the ones I know are really praise songs—like "Praise God From Whom All Blessings Flow."

ELLEN: Right. And now here is this *(lifts out Bible and holds it up)*.

CHILD: Of course! Reading and studying the Bible honors God.

CHILD: And that's a big part of our worship services.

ELLEN: Prayer, too, comes from it. We learn to pray from the Bible and we can pray God's Word back to God as we worship.

CHILD: I never thought of that. What do you mean "pray God's Word back to God?"

CHILD: Oh, I know! My Sunday school teacher talked about that. It's saying a Bible verse in your prayer. Like one we learned is—let me think—oh yeah, "I will exalt you, my God the King; I will praise your name for ever and ever." *Psalm 145:1 NIV*

ELLEN: That's good. Now I have one more thing in the box *(lifts out some musical instrument—may be as simple as a tambourine)* You know this!

CHILD: Music!

CHILD: Joyful sounds!

ELLEN: Right. We worship God with music, too. Well, we can't really wrap up praise and worship, but we can give it to Jesus for his birthday—and all year long.

CHILD: How about let's give him praise in song right now?

           (Children sing song of praise.)

NATHAN: My sister got to show you her idea for a birthday present for Jesus first. Now here's mine! *(Pulls large package to center of group.)*

CHILD: What's in that big box?

NATHAN: Just a minute. You remember our Sunday school teacher said that Jesus came to bring peace to all the earth?

CHILD: Yeah, but there isn't peace everywhere yet.

NATHAN: That's true and that's another gift we can give Jesus.

CHILD: You've lost me!

NATHAN: We can pray for peace and we can show by our actions that we believe in peace. If everyone tried live as Jesus wants us to live, the world, will become a peaceful place.

CHILD: So how can we do that? What did you put in your package?

NATHAN: *(lifts out articles as he refers to them)* Here's a framed copy of the Ten Commandments so we can hang it up somewhere. It will remind us of what God wants us to do. And here are some knee pads.

CHILD: Knee pads? What are those for?

NATHAN: Think about it. We should start by praying for peace. It won't hurt us to spend some time on our knees.

CHILD: Awright, Nathan! Your present is something Jesus wants for his birthday and one we can keep on giving.

CHILD: Let's sing something about peace. Do we know anything?

           (Children sing.)

CHILD: I guess we can give birthday gifts to Jesus!

CHILD: Sure. I never thought of praise or living a peaceful life as gifts. Isn't it great!

CHILD: Great! I wish I'd thought of a present to bring.

CHILD: Well, we can all give the things Ellen and Nathan talked about.

ELLEN: My other brother has a gift to show us too. Come on, Dan. Let everyone see your package.

DAN: *(comes to center with wrapped gift)* You may think its corny, but here it is. *(Holds up package with* LOVE *on it.)*

           (chorus of children exclaiming such as "Why didn't I think of that!" "Awesome" "Sure, that's a great gift!" etc.)

DAN: We use this word—love—all the time when we don't really mean it. We say we love french fries—

CHILD: And ice cream—

CHILD: And soccer!

DAN: But Jesus said to love God and love others and that sums up Christian living.

CHILD: Must be a different kind of love!

DAN: My dad says it means "reverent affection."

CHILD: Do you feel that kind of love?

DAN: Dad said if we act like we love—the feelings will follow.

CHILD: How do we "act like" we love God?

DAN: Let me show you what's in my package. First, here's a Bible so we can learn about God—how to love God—how to accept what Jesus did for us. Then, here's a book with coupons my family members can redeem. Each one says I'll do something for them. We learn to show love to our family and that honors God.

CHILD: Cool. It's hard to show love for my sister!

CHILD: Or my brother!

DAN: Here's a clock—to check up on ourselves and how we use our time. Do we have time for TV and computer games but not for Bible study? What do we love? This is just a start. I know you can think of lots of things for your "Love for Jesus" birthday package.

CHILD: I think I'll make one and put it under the Christmas tree!

CHILD: Me, too!

DAN: Here's a verse I wrote for this present:

We love 'cause God loves us from above.
God gave the greatest gift to everyone
When God sent Jesus to share his love.
Happy Birthday to Jesus, God's Son!

CHILD: Awesome, Dan!

ELLEN: Now we all have ideas of what to give Jesus for his birthday.

(Children begin to rise with exclamations like "thanks for the party," "Merry Christmas," "I'm going to give Jesus presents," and so on. May exit singing "Happy Birthday" again or group together for a final Christmas carol.)

WHAT THE ANIMALS MADE KNOWN

by Judy Gattis Smith

Production Notes

This play gives third and fourth grade children a chance to use their artistic imaginations by creating masks for all the characters. If you have more children than characters in the play, have more than one child take the part of some animals.

Paper plates are simple and inexpensive and masks made from them can be created quickly. They can be made more elaborately if you wish.

Materials Needed

> white paper plates
> tempera paints mixed with water
> paint brushes
> felt-tip markers
> construction paper in a variety of colors
> scissors
> pencils
> glitter
> glue
> fake fur cloth scraps
> craft sticks
> masking tape
> white cotton balls

1. Cut eye holes in the plates before you give them to the children.

2. Use tempera paints or felt-tip markers to color the masks. For example: use gray for the donkey, tan for the ox, browns and tans for the owl, and so on. Leave the sheep mask

white, but use a black felt-tip marker to draw curls to resemble tufts of wool. If you have fake fur cloth scraps, cover the masks for the donkey and the ox. If you have cotton balls glue them to the mask for the sheep.

3. Cover the lightening bug mask with glue and sprinkle glitter over the glue.

4. Use a black felt- tip marker to draw features such as a nose and mouth for the donkey and ox. Circle the eyes on all masks in black, or cut circles from black cloth or paper scraps and glue them on.

5. Cut brightly colored construction paper feathers for the bird, and glue them to the top edge of the bird's mask.

6. Draw a wavy rooster's comb on bright orange construction paper, cut it out, and glue it to the top of the rooster's mask.

7. Draw two horns on tan construction paper for the ox, cut them out, and glue them on the ox's mask.

8. Draw two donkey's ears on gray construction paper, cut them out, and glue them on the donkey's mask.

9. For the beaks of the bird, owl, and rooster, cut a 2″ by 2″ square yellow construction paper. Fold it diagonally so that two points meet. Glue the bottom of the triangle to the puppet's face where the beak goes.

10. Color the mask for the bee with yellow and black stripes.

11. Use masking tape to attach a craft stick to the bottom of each mask to use as a handle.

Characters

Narrator
Little Bird
Donkey
Ox
Bees
Lightening Bugs
Rooster
Owl
Sheep

NARRATOR: Once upon a time there was a little bird—a lonely little bird.

(Little Bird comes on stage.)

NARRATOR: Little Bird sometimes flew far and wide, but mostly Little Bird circled a small territory, always just looking for food.

(Little Bird moves slowly in large circles, sighs.)

NARRATOR: The territory included an ordinary stable, rather dull and colorless. But sometimes there would be a bit of grain or a crumb from a stable boy's lunch. Little Bird circled. Little Bird ate. Little Bird slept. But Little Bird never sang.

(Little Bird pantomimes eating and sleeping.)

NARRATOR: Then one night as Little Bird flew over the stable, she noticed something wondrous. She flew closer. Warmth and light radiated from the stable.

(Little Bird moves closer to the stable.)

LITTLE BIRD: What has happened here?

NARRATOR: The air was filled with gentleness and love. The stable creatures tried to answer Little Bird's question.

DONKEY: It was a long, tiring journey. There were rough roads, steep hills, and the weight of a weary mother.

NARRATOR: But the donkey's words sounded like:

DONKEY: Clop—Clop—Good News—Good News.

OX: Mary and Joseph were turned away from the crowded inn, so they came to stay in this stable. During the night, Mary gave birth.

NARRATOR: But swaying and stomping, the ox sounded like:

OX: Marvel-Marvel-Marvelous.

BEES: People have waited for hundreds of years for a Savior to be born, someone to show what God is like.

NARRATOR: But they could only hum:

BEES: The Lord has comemmmm.

SHEEP: The newborn baby was wrapped in bands of cloth. Then he was gently laid in our manger.

NARRATOR: But the sheep could only bleat:

SHEEP:	Blessed—Blessed.
LIGHTENING BUGS:	The sky was filled with angels.
NARRATOR:	But the bugs could only flicker:
LIGHTENING BUGS:	Glory—Glory—Glory.
ROOSTER:	The baby would be the Savior of the world.
NARRATOR:	But the rooster could only crow:
ROOSTER:	Do-doodle-do. He comes for you.
NARRATOR:	Each animal, in its own way and with its own voice, told a part of the Christmas story.
	(All animals make their sounds at the same time.)
NARRATOR:	Little Bird understood, but when she opened her throat to join in, there was no song.
LITTLE BIRD:	Why can't I sing? Why can't I join in?
NARRATOR:	A wise owl near the stable roof sensed Little Bird's desire to sing.
OWL:	Who-o-o could sing? You can only sing about someone or something that you love. Who-o-om do you love?
LITTLE BIRD:	Love? What is love? *(looking around)* But there is something special in this stable. I feel it. It must be love. Rejoice!

NARRATOR: Little Bird's throat opened in glorious song. Her music flooded the rafters. After that miraculous night Little Bird flew far and wide, singing about the Savior's birth.

(Sing Stanzas 1 and 3 of "Love Came Down at Christmas.")

NOTES